PIANO • VOCAL • GUITAR

SOME NIGHTS BY FUN.

ISBN 978-1-4768-2247-1

HAL•LEONARD® CORPORATION

7777 W. BLUEMOUND RD. P.O. BOX 13819 MILWAUKEE, WI 53213

Visit Hal Leonard Online at
www.halleonard.com

SOME NIGHTS (INTRO)

Words and Music by JEFF BHASKER,
ANDREW DOST, JACK ANTONOFF
and NATE RUESS

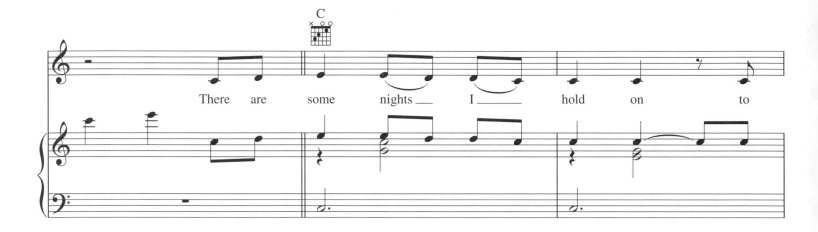

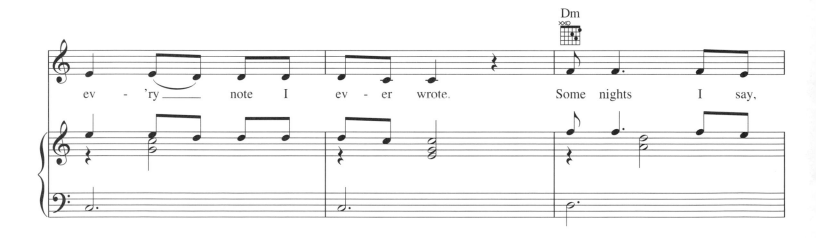

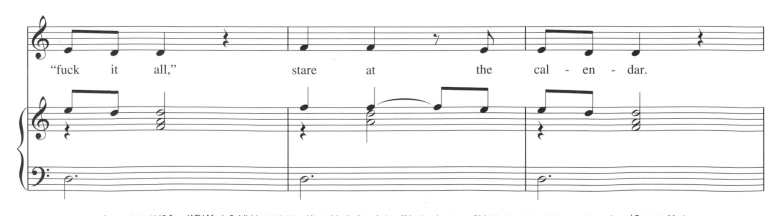

Spoken: *And you have every right to be scared.*

Late - ly I been go - in' cra - zy. And
Late - ly I been fuck - ing cra -

zy. There are some nights I wait ___ for some - one to

save us but I nev - er look in - ward, try not to look

up - ward. And some nights I pray ___ a sign is gon - na

SOME NIGHTS

Words and Music by JEFF BHASKER,
ANDREW DOST, JACK ANTONOFF
and NATE RUESS

Moderately, with a March feel

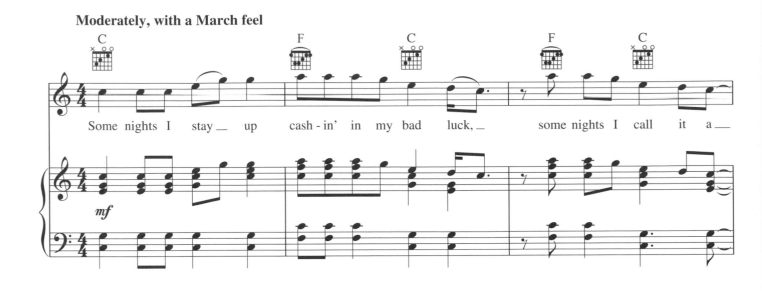

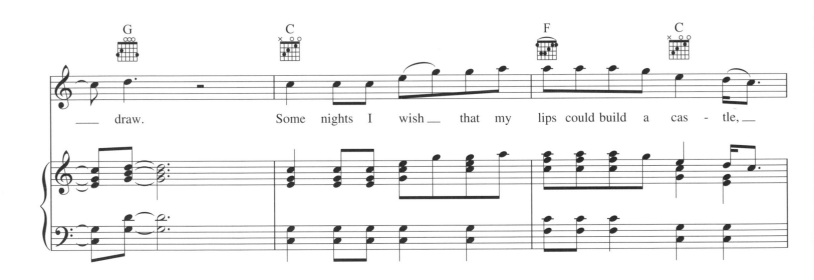

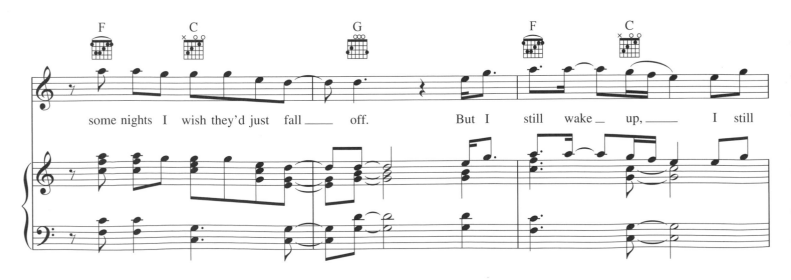

To Coda

19

WE ARE YOUNG

Words and Music by JEFF BHASKER,
ANDREW DOST, JACK ANTONOFF
and NATE RUESS

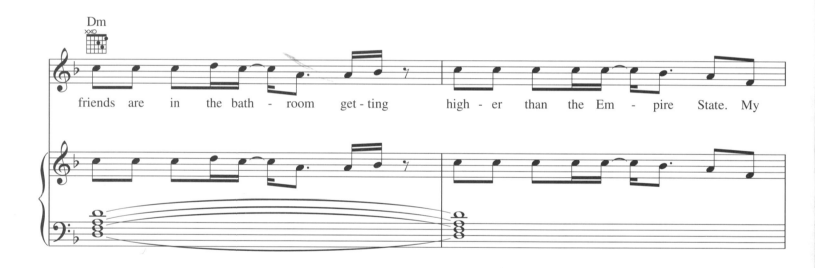

tak - en by some sun - glass - es ask - ing 'bout a scar. __ And I know I gave it to you

months a - go; __ I know you're try - ing to for - get. __ But be-

tween the drinks and sub - tle things, the holes in my a - pol - o - gies, __ you know

I'm try - ing hard to take __ it __ back. So, if by the time the bar clos - es and you

Suddenly slower

CARRY ON

Words and Music by JEFF BHASKER,
ANDREW DOST, JACK ANTONOFF
and NATE RUESS

IT GETS BETTER

Words and Music by JEFF BHASKER,
ANDREW DOST, JACK ANTONOFF
and NATE RUESS

WHY AM I THE ONE

Words and Music by JEFF BHASKER,
ANDREW DOST, JACK ANTONOFF
and NATE RUESS

Moderately slow groove

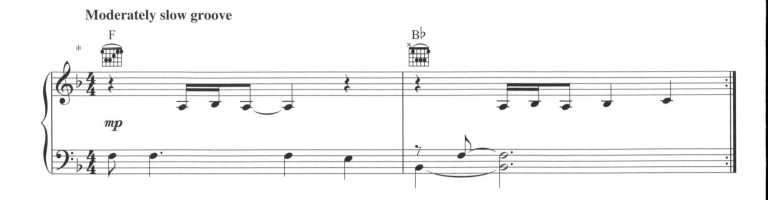

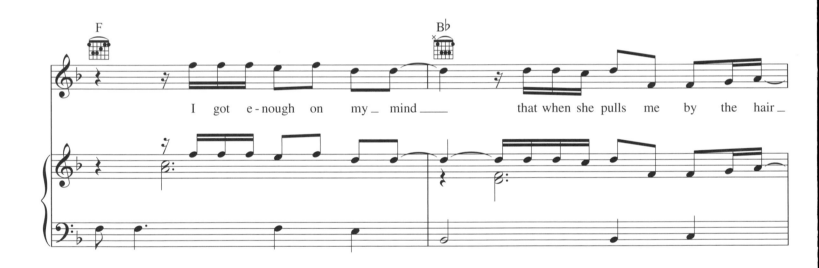

I got e-nough on my mind ___ that when she pulls me by the hair ___

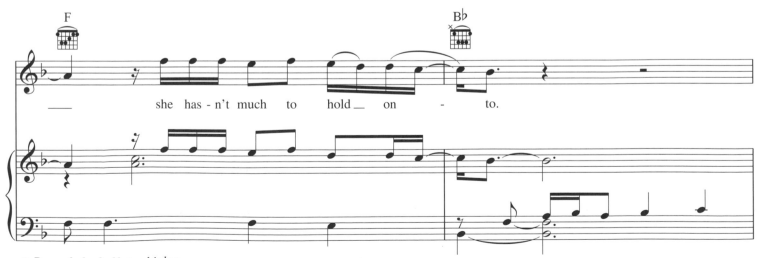

___ she has-n't much to hold ___ on - to.

* Recorded a half step higher.

For once, for once, for once _ I get the feel-in' that I'm right where I be-long._____

Why am I _____ the one _____ al-ways pack-ing up _____ my stuff? _____ I

think I kind - a like _____ it but _____ I might-a had _____ too

much. I'll move back down _____ to this

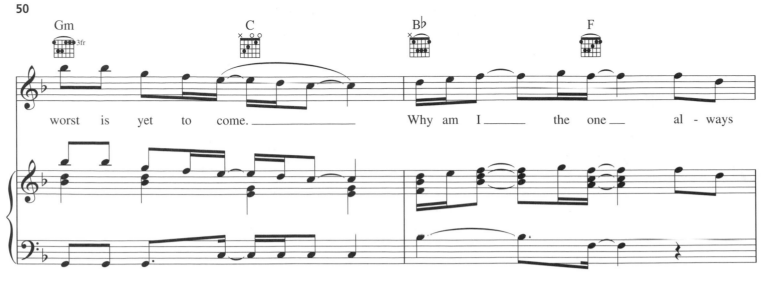

worst is yet to come. _____ Why am I ____ the one ___ al - ways

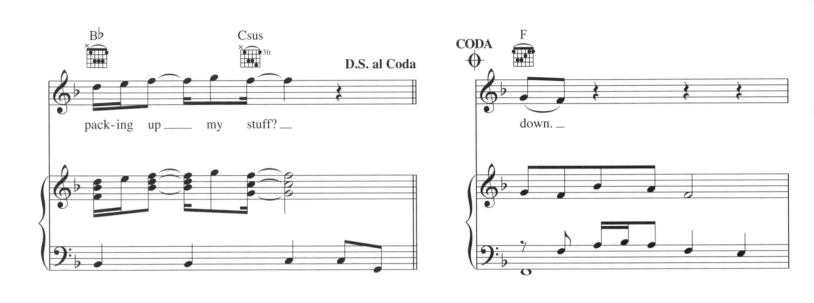

pack-ing up ___ my stuff? ___

D.S. al Coda

CODA

down. ___

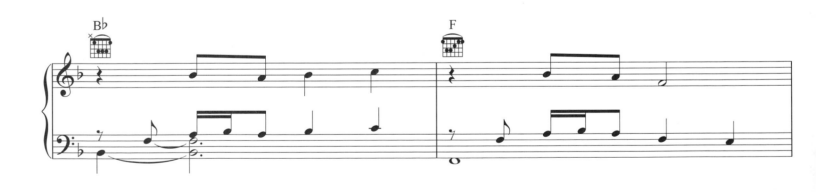

ALL ALONE

Words and Music by JEFF BHASKER,
ANDREW DOST, JACK ANTONOFF
and NATE RUESS

Moderate Pop Rock

I fell in love with a wind-up sou-ve-nir. ___

I bought it down-town as I was on my way to meet ___ you.

She sounds like the songs you used to sing to put me to sleep. ___

ALL ALRIGHT

Words and Music by JEFF BHASKER,
JAKE DUTTON, ANDREW DOST,
JACK ANTONOFF, NATE RUESS
and EMILE HAYNIE

Moderate Pop Anthem

Yeah, it's all al-right, I guess it's all al-right.

I've got noth-ing left in-side of my chest but it's all al-right.

D

E

F#m

see you burn-ing out. And I know, oh no, that

C#m

Bm

D/A

I put up a front, but may-be just this once,

D

E

A

let me keep this one. _____ And it's all al-right,

C#m/G#

F#m

I guess it's all al-right. _____ I've got noth-ing left in-

side of my chest but it's all al - right. ___ Yeah, it's all al - right, ___

___ I guess it's all al - right. ___ I've got noth - ing left in -

side of my chest, but it's all al - right. ___

ONE FOOT

Words and Music by ANDREW DOST,
JACK ANTONOFF, NATE RUESS
and EMILE HAYNIE

Oh, oh, oh, I don't need a new love or a new life, just a bet-ter place to

die. ___ I

hap-pened to stum-ble u-pon ___ a cha-pel last ___ night. And I

can't help but back up when I think of what hap-pens in - side. ___ I got

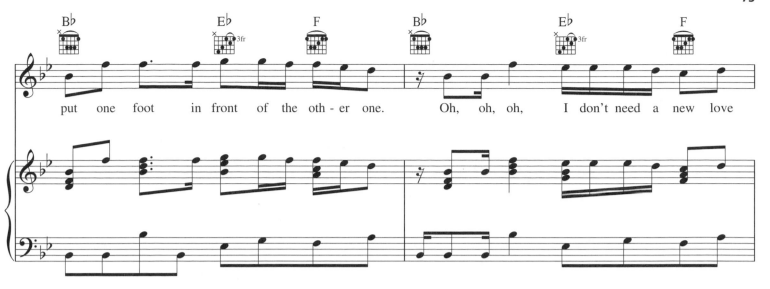

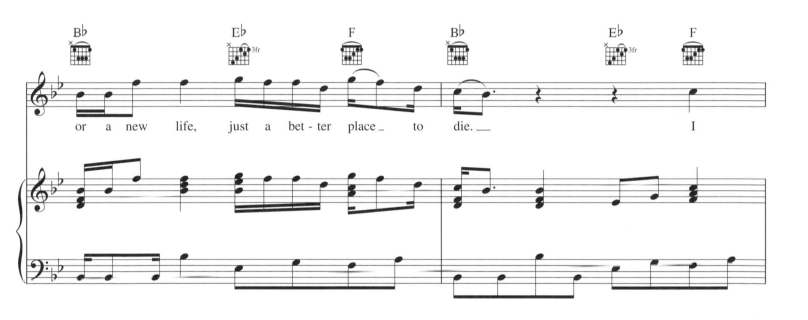

or a new life, just a bet - ter place __ to die. __

In front of the oth - er one. In front of the oth - er one.

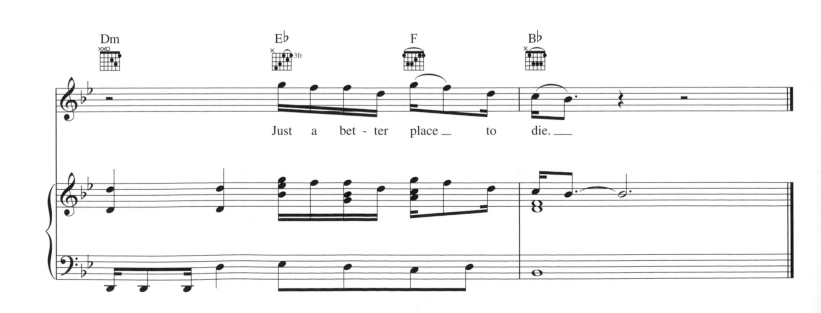

Just a bet - ter place __ to die. __

STARS

Words and Music by JEFF BHASKER,
ANDREW DOST, JACK ANTONOFF
and NATE RUESS

the boats _ and past _ loves that flew a - way _ or start - ed sink - in.' And it's

cra - zy here with-out _ you, I used to think _ this all _ was ours. _ We stay up late, _

_ de - bate _ on how we _ find _ our way. You say, "It's all up in the stars." _

Well, some nights I rule the world _ with bar lights and _

OUT ON THE TOWN

Words and Music by ANDREW DOST,
JACK ANTONOFF, NATE RUESS
and EMILE HAYNIE

Moderate Rock